CW00540686

"Divine Madness"

JOSEF PIEPER

"Divine Madness"

Plato's Case against Secular Humanism

Translated by Lothar Krauth

IGNATIUS PRESS   SAN FRANCISCO

Title of the German original:
"Göttlicher Wahnsinn"
Eine Platon-Interpretation
© 1989 Schwabenverlag AG
Ostfildern/Stuttgart, Germany

Cover by Roxanne Mei Lum

© 1995 Ignatius Press, San Francisco
ISBN 978-0-89870-557-7
Library of Congress catalogue number 95-75667
Printed in the United States of America

Contents

ESTABLISHING THE THEME

"THE HIGHEST GOODS come to us in the manner of the *mania*, inasmuch as the same is bestowed on us as a divine gift." This pronouncement by Socrates—with its central term *mania* remaining untranslated for now—contains an entire world view; it proclaims above all a fundamental opinion about the meaning of human existence. It shows that man is indeed of such a kind as to possess his own self in freedom and self-determination, that he is able and also obliged to examine critically everything he encounters, that he is above all able and obliged to determine, based on insight, his own life. Yet it further indicates that man, at the same time, is in his personal selfhood integrated into the whole of reality in such a way that he can very well be shaken out of his self-possession, and this not only in the form of forced oppression but possibly, so long as man on his part does not barricade himself in refusal, also in such a form that *in the very loss of self-possession* there is bestowed on him a fulfillment not achieved in any other way.

This concept of man, with the tension of its structure, can of course never be captured in some smooth formula; its inherent explosive potential indicates, rather, an implacable and disturbing challenge. And this concept of man, in a unique way, occupied Plato's mind all his life. Yet he was far from placing his emphasis on the same aspect. Like every true philosopher, he was concerned not so much with finding some satisfying and handy formula as with not overlooking anything. Thus he never denied or disregarded the fact that *both aspects* are essential to man, self-possession as well as its loss through the irruption of a higher power. But he was not always disposed to interpret such loss of self-directed autonomy as a gain.

In his earlier writings, he seems inclined to call the state of "being-beside-oneself-in-enthusiasm" a "sickness", even though he would have considered it a worse sickness *not* to be able to be "sick" in such a way. ("The sickness that consists in the inability to be sick"—this expression of modern psychology comes to mind.)

The following reflections are an attempt to interpret primarily the late Dialogue *Phaedrus*. In this Dialogue, Socrates discusses four different forms of the *theia mania*, by which he means precisely this god-given state of "being-beside-oneself".

PROPHECY

THE FIRST DISCUSSION concerns prophetic ecstasy,
"divination" in the strict sense, the *transport prophé-
tique*. Three figures are identified by name: the
prophetess at Delphi, the priestesses of Dodona, and
the Sibyl. They all have in common that, while
they were in a state of ecstatic frenzy, they accomplished great things through their utterances, but,
when they were of clear mind and calm self-
possession, they were unable to say anything important.

At the time of Socrates, Delphi had been a sanc-
tuary for more than a thousand years, extending its
influence far into Asia and Egypt. Regardless of the
interpretation of details, we now know that the
effects of the Delphian Oracle, especially when
aimed at the political arena, can hardly be overesti-
mated. Its oracles contained religious and ethical

demands found practically nowhere else in the pre-Christian world formulated with such consistency and intensity. For example, not only is the inviolable right to asylum proclaimed here, and not only is the custom of the blood feud denounced, but the earliest rules for a more humane conduct of war, indeed for some kind of "international law", can also be traced back to the Delphian Oracle.

The most ancient formulaic hymnic wisdom of the Greek religion originated with the priestesses of Dodona in northern Greece: "Zeus was, Zeus is, and Zeus will ever be—O Zeus, thou art most powerful!" All too easily do we tend to overlook such things in favor of those entertaining stories about the gods of the Homeric mythology, stories that Plato dismisses as a perversion of the true divine doctrine—according to the *Greek* conception, of course.

And finally, the Sibyl. The most ancient testimony known to us derives from one of the great pre-Socratic philosophers, Heraclitus; it is itself cast in Sibylline obscurity: "The Sibyl, with raging lips uttering things unamusing, and unadorned, and unanointed, resounds through the millennia, driven by the god."

Plato's contemporaries are so familiar with all this that the text states explicitly: Let us not talk at

length about things known to everybody. And
then, recapitulating, the text says it would be good
to reflect on the fact that the ancients, who gave
names to all things, assigned to this oracular art of
the seer-priestess and the Sibyl the name *mania* as a
name of *honor*. A few lines later, this title is confirmed once again: the ancient ones testified that
more venerable than human reasonableness is the
theia mania, the god-given and enthusiastic state of
being-beside-oneself.

We latter-day readers of Plato are at first inclined
to connect the Platonic commentary on the prophetic trance only with Delphi, Dodona, and the
Sibyl, therefore with the "history of Greek religion"—and thus to let it rest. Surveying the aca-
demic literature on Plato, we are largely confirmed
and encouraged in this approach. But in doing this
we deprive ourselves of the genuine gain we might
very well derive from studying Plato's words or
even simply reading them attentively. I am re-
minded here of C. S. Lewis' *Screwtape Letters*. A
devil called "Screwtape", grown "wise" through
extensive experience, imparts instructions and advice to his nephew, inexperienced in the ways of
humans, in letters expressing a philosophical anthro-
pology altogether as humorous as it is profound but,

of course, turned upside down. One of Screwtape's letters deals with studying the ancients:

"Only the learned read old books, and we [the united demons of hell] have now so dealt with the learned that they are of all men the least likely to acquire wisdom by doing so. We have done this by inculcating The Historical Point of View. Put briefly, The Historical Point of View means that when a learned man is presented with any statement in an ancient author, the one question he never asks is whether it is true. He asks who influenced the ancient writer, and how far the statement is consistent with what he said in other books, and what phase in the writer's development, or in the general history of thought, it illustrates, and how it affected later writers, and how often it was misunderstood (specially by the learned man's own colleagues) . . .", and so forth.

But as soon as I, in view of Plato's comments on the first form of enthusiastic being-beside-oneself, pose the question whether something is stated here that describes the reality of a situation; whether something comes to the fore here that in actual fact is found in the reality of the human essence—then it immediately becomes impossible to confine Plato's testimony merely to the history of Greek religion. Such a question right away sweeps aside the *narrow category* of being merely something of the past.

For example, although the modern-day Christian has encountered the Sibyl in the sequence *Dies Irae*, right in the middle of the Church's [former] funeral liturgy, where she is mentioned in one breath with the biblical king David, both prophetically testifying to the catastrophic end of history (*teste David cum Sibylla*), this connection may still be taken as a quaint flowery ornament without any particular implication. In order to address seriously the question of the truth of it all, we have to translate Plato's words and meaning more resolutely into our own mental framework.

Incidentally, there does exist such a "translation", dating from pre-Christian times, into a language closer to ours: the language of the Romans, Latin. In the sixth book of the *Aeneid*, which contains a description of Aeneas consulting the Sibyl of Cumae, the *theia mania* is indeed presented as "sacred frenzy": In the enormous cavern of Cumae, perforated a hundred times and having a hundred mouths that carry "with rushing voices" the responses of the Sibyl, there she herself stood at the entrance, and, as she spoke,

> . . . neither her face
> Nor hue went untransformed, nor did her hair
> Stay neatly bound; her breast heaved, her wild heart
> Grew large with passion. Taller to their eyes
> And sounding now no longer like a mortal
> Since she had felt the god's power breathing near
> . . . Apollo
> Pulled her up raging, or else whipped her on,
> Digging the spurs beneath her breast.

Even so, I would not yet call this a translation into terms familiar to us. Instead, this is accomplished through one single word used by Virgil. It appears in the first verses of the same book, where it is said about the Sibyl that the Delian god Apollo "breathed into her the richness of the spirit". The name for this "breath", of course, is *inspiratio*, inspiration!

In reference to this word we are now able to take the testimony found in the Platonic Dialogue *Phaedrus* and reformulate it in contemporary and more specific terms. Human nature is so positioned within its existential realm as to be essentially open toward the sphere of the divine. Man is constituted in such a way that, on the one hand, he needs to be forced, through inspiration, out of the self-sufficiency of his thinking—through an event, therefore, that lies beyond his disposing power, an event that comes to him only in the form of something unpredictable. On the other hand, it is precisely in this loss of rational sovereignty that man gains a wealth, above all, of intuition, light, truth, and insight into reality, all of which would otherwise remain beyond his reach. Here we are explicitly looking not at the results of human genius but at the effects of a different, a loftier, a divine power. Such overwhelming inspiration is possible not only in the abstract; it really happens every now and then. Whenever it does happen, it happens in such a way that the *sophrosýne* [self-possession], as well as everything implied by it, is being forcefully suspended, no matter how much the dignity of the human person is ordinarily based on it. Inspiration as an event occurs in the form of being-beside-oneself, a *theia mania*—hence that inspiration likewise appears to "the multitude" as madness.

It is immediately obvious that such a statement invites discussion of the metaphysical structure of man's nature, which lies all but beyond the grasp of "science". He who would discuss the truth of this discourse has to be prepared to declare his ultimate convictions. That is, to put it briefly and in blunt terms, a Christian, confronted with such statements and pursuing a philosophical interpretation of Plato, cannot easily escape the necessity of including in the discussion teachings of the Christian faith. These teachings, for their part, clearly agree with Plato that, indeed, the limitations of man's nature, as well as its infinite openness and capacity—both together—are manifest in the occurrence of revelatory divine inspiration.

The question remains, of course, whether this agreement might also extend to the specific ways and means of revelation and inspiration. Could a Christian theologian really accept Plato's talk of enthusiastic being-beside-oneself or even his talk of *mania*, no matter how often it be declared a "*divine* madness"? How, in any case, does Christian theology conceive of revelation and inspiration as an event happening to the first recipient?

I have to admit that I expected, compared with Plato's description of the *theia mania*, an answer much more composed and, as it were, more detached, more rationally unimpassioned. But then I encountered, to my surprise, almost literally the same description of the revelatory event, as found in Plato's *Phaedrus*, in Thomas Aquinas, whom no one could accuse of a lack of sobriety.

Thomas discusses the instance of revelation and inspiration under the heading of *prophetia* and *raptus*. The very term *raptus*, having a clearly discernible connotation of something intrusive and violent, is obviously not far removed from *theia mania*. This connection is confirmed immediately by Scholasticism's definition, quoted by Thomas: "being lifted up through a higher power, away from those things that pertain to nature, and toward those things that are against nature" (*in id quod est contra naturam*). Prophecy as well, seen as an event in the mind of the one who experiences revelation and inspiration, is described by Thomas in terms not only of *passio* but even of "failure, giving way". He asks, for instance, whether *prophetia* is a *habitus*, belonging to the "prophet" like a possession, a talent, a skill. He answers: No, the prophetic light appears in the prophet's soul as a reception or a "fleeting engraving. . . . Prophecy, insofar as it refers to the seeing on the part of the prophet, is in a certain sense admittedly a mental action; but in reference to the light that is received suddenly and in the manner of something passing through ('like the sun's light in the atmosphere'), it is something received. . . .

"In the process of prophetic revelation, the prophet's mind is being moved by the Holy Spirit like an instrument that submits. . . ." And, finally, it is an entirely unexpected discovery that Thomas, the accepted model of the most unimpassioned rationality, declares cognition during sleep to be more powerful as regards receptivity than the cognition of one who is awake—thus positioning himself by one single surprising step squarely on Plato's side. Rationalism, however, because it distorts the entire reality of human life, necessarily finds both thinkers equally incomprehensible and inaccessible.

"CATHARSIS"

THE SECOND FORM of divinely caused being-beside-
oneself discussed by Socrates has been characterized
as "cathartic mania". Any comparison and connection with certain tenets we ourselves deem true is
possible, of course, only if we hold an opinion at all
regarding the topic considered here. At first sight,
we seem not to have such an opinion. What, then,
is meant by the term "cathartic mania"? First of all,
what does the text say? The passage in the Dialogue
Phaedrus reads thus:

> Again, for those sore plagues and dire afflictions,
> which you are aware lingered in certain families as
> the wraith of some old ancestral guilt, *mania* devised
> a remedy, after it had entered into the heart of the
> proper persons, and to the proper persons revealed
> its secrets; for it fled for refuge to prayer and ser-
> vices of the gods, and thence obtaining purifications

and atoning rites made its possessor whole for time
present and time to come, by showing him the way
of escape from the evils that encompassed him, if
only he were rightly frenzied and possessed.

On this point, the literature on Plato offers only
some extremely meager and stammering words. Wilamowitz candidly declares this to be "not understood" as yet: "Nowhere did I find an explanation,
and I am at a loss myself." Of course, one could pro-
pose simply to disregard this matter altogether if it
were not rather vexing that we should be so utterly
incapable of recognizing as meaningful, that is, as
connected to reality, a thesis pronounced by Plato
with obviously serious intent. This would be disturbing not so much because of the gap in interpretation,
irking to the historian and philologist, but rather
because we would have reason to suspect that we
have developed a blind spot as regards reality, if we in
fact—confronted with such a specific pronouncement, which Plato evidently deemed fundamental—
do not understand at all what he is talking about.

At this point, two questions should be asked.
First: Looking at our current total knowledge of
man, is there in it something that corresponds to
what Plato called "those sore plagues and dire
afflictions", rooted "in some old ancestral guilt"?

Some translations (e.g., K. Hildebrandt) also say, "flowing from an ancient curse"; *ménima*, indeed, means both: guilt and (divine) wrath. The most appropriate term, combining both elements, may be the German *Verhängnis* [doom]. The second question: Looking at our knowledge of man, is there in it something that corresponds to what Plato says about the divinely appointed *mania*, which he declares to be alone able to relieve man of such an ancient burden? Only if such corresponding elements exist will we be at all prepared to understand what Plato is talking about here; above all, only then can we apply Plato's discourse to those notions we ourselves deem true.

Concerning the first question, we should recognize at once that the ailments, burdens, afflictions, plagues, and miseries mentioned by Plato are obviously not, or not primarily, to be seen as physical infirmities, sufferings, and wounds but rather as burdens of the soul, which oppress and darken the heart.

One contemporary commentary on the *Phaedrus* Dialogue holds that Plato probably was thinking of something like the story of Orestes, who is haunted by the avenging specters, the *Eumenides* [Erinnyes]. But it is not only in the tragedies of antiquity that we encounter these *Eumenides*. The modern-day

spectator can watch them appear, in T. S. Eliot's
Family Reunion, as the chorus stepping out of the
window alcoves of a contemporary English country
manor:

> And whether in Argos or England,
> There are certain inflexible laws
> Unalterable, in the nature of music.

It is, of course, less important to find agreement in
vocabulary than in the matter itself. Regarding the
subject matter here, we should recall, for instance,
the findings of modern psychoanalysis. These
findings, indeed, did not bring to light any totally
independent and "new" insights. On the contrary,
they simply confirmed to a large extent those things
already known and uttered since ancient days by
renowned authorities on the human heart and in
sapiential traditions of nations. These findings con-
firm this, too: In the life of the soul there are indeed
burdens, tribulations, and ailments that can be
shown to flow "from ancient doom", in which the
afflicted individuals themselves, as well as preceding
generations, are caught up in some unspecified par-
ticipation, and in which, moreover, a certain inner
corruption, impossible to define, coincides with an
inescapable and fateful external destiny. In short, any

reflection on the totality of man's existence will even today lead to the insight that such burdens, flowing from such roots, are real.

Furthermore, this insight suggests that man is unable to free himself from these burdens by means of mere rational technique; that, on the contrary, such an attempt would render the burden even more burdensome. Liberation can occur only through a process of healing characterized, at least negatively, by the necessity for the one desiring healing to relinquish temporarily the steering wheel of rational self-control and self-possession. Indeed, it is not some busily pursued activity that is here in order but, on the contrary, a willingness to submit to being led and affected—for instance, by delving to the domain of the unconscious and of dreams.

Plato was no doubt aware that Asclepius' healing art originally had a magical character, offering the supplicant advice and healing in dreams. A dream, however, is something we do not originate ourselves. "We suffer a dream." This sentence is not an ancient pronouncement; its author is none other than C. G. Jung. Like Plato, he too mentions the necessity, for the sake of healing and restoration, of abandoning oneself to a state of being-beside-oneself, of *mania*; and he quotes here the "ancient oracle: 'Let go of what you possess, and so you shall receive.'" The gift of receiving, then, has been given the same name in modern psychology as in Platonic teaching: the gift of cleansing, *catharsis*.

Against this attempt to draw an analogy between Plato on the one hand and modern psychoanalysis on the other, one could certainly object as follows: No matter how much the "liberation of the sub-conscious" in modern parlance might resemble the "being-beside-oneself" of the Platonic *mania*, the decisive point for Plato consists in its being a *divinely caused* "being-beside-oneself", a *theia mania*; and regarding this the theory of the subconscious does not utter a word!

As much as this objection is justified in view of the explicitly declared or, rather, explicitly unde-clared position of modern psychoanalysis, I would try to counter it with this question: Inasmuch as the soul itself certainly knows its wants and needs, does not this soul's existential foundation, lying beyond any rational calculation, at least silently intimate the possibility of a supernatural, divinely created origin also of the healing process? Man, by letting go of himself, does not at all abandon himself into the realm of what is merely "irrational". He enters the healing darkness of his own divine origin.

One more aspect should be mentioned here. Plato, if he really had in mind the story of Orestes, the matricide, could have understood the burden "rooted in ancestral guilt" specifically as guilt in the literal sense of the word or, at least, as including such personal guilt. In that case, his thesis would assert that guilt, crime, and sin cannot be undone and that we cannot get rid of such burdens simply through a rational program of inner discipline or through some external regimen, no matter how sublime. Guilt is wiped out by means of the *theia mania*.

Contemporary man, however, if he is a Christian (once again, here the ultimate existential roots have to be brought into the discourse and not only when agreement prevails but also in the face of disagreement!), can hardly avoid taking Plato's side and speaking of his own conviction, which likewise asserts that guilt can be absolved only through *metánoia*, through repentance and conversion. *Metánoia* means, first, that one surrenders and abandons the self-sufficiency of a mind that claims total independence. *Metánoia* is precisely the opposite of the attitude, defined by Seneca and spanning the centuries, that it is the fruit of philosophy "never to regret anything". Second, the notion of *metánoia* implies that such conversion can never be fully decided by a mere act of the will; rather, it is bestowed on man as a divine favor.

POESY

THE THIRD FORM of divinely prompted being-beside-oneself discussed by Socrates is the poetic *mania*, the ecstasy inspired by the Muses and seizing "upon a tender and virgin soul, stirring it to rapturous frenzy". And a clear note of caution is added immediately: Genuine and grand poetry is not possible unless born out of divine madness. Whosoever wishes to be a poet by his own devices will never experience the blessed initiation. The poetry of those who are reasonable and sensible fades into obscurity before the poetry of those who speak in the ecstasy of being-beside-oneself.

"How can this recognition of poetry . . . stand side by side with the condemnation found in the *Republic*, which would ban Homer and Tragedy from the ideal commonwealth?" This observation (by Wilamowitz) appears again and again in the lit-

erature on Plato in different variations. There may
be no real problem lurking here at all. All along, as
in the Dialogue *Meno*, which was written much earlier than the *Republic*, Plato distinguished between
"divine poets" and those who have no claim to this
title. Among those other, non-divine, poets, he evidently counts also Homer, because Homer attrib-
utes ungodly things to the gods.

Genuine poesy, then, originates with divine inspiration; it flows from a condition of the soul closer
to a state of being-beside-oneself than possessing-
oneself; and this being-beside-oneself is not the
result of wine, poison, or some other drug but is
caused by some higher power. Poesy, if it is true
poesy, flows from "enthusiasm" in the strict sense of
the word.

Can we moderns look at this Platonic thesis in
any way other than merely historically? After we
consider everything we know scientifically about
psychological requisites and other relevant conditions for poetic creation and artistic production as
such, can we still seriously assert that poetry flows
from divine inspiration?

In this context, "we" does not mean simply contemporary man in general but, above all, the Christian. Can a Christian accept a thesis that puts poesy

on the same level as revelation and inspiration? In a biography on Rilke we read: "Rilke is the quintessential figure of a poet, in the simple sense of being a vessel for divine inspiration. One necessarily has to believe this in order to do justice to Rilke." You do not have to lack a poetic inclination, after all, or be specifically unsympathetic toward Rilke, to consider such words as, at the least, romantic exaggeration, if not simply blasphemy. And yet, does not Plato say the very same thing?

The reflection here points out the sad deficiency of our not having available any theological or philosophical doctrine on the nature of the fine arts, which would provide the framework for discussing Plato's thesis in more adequate critical terms. Such a theology or philosophy of poetics, incidentally, might have to be reconstructed ever anew, according to the different spiritual conditions of each epoch; and this would probably turn out to be, like theology and philosophy in general, a task becoming ever more difficult.

Reinhold Schneider, shortly before his death, stated that he never ceased searching for the nature of poesy but that, in his experience, "as the years go by, it becomes more and more difficult to find an answer". To pursue this question here is, of course,

impossible. At this point of our *Phaedrus* interpretation, however, we must emphasize one particular
aspect: In spite of all "scientific" analyses of poetry;
in spite of all the superficial popular success of manifest pseudo-poetry (no matter whether it presents
itself as literary art or politically engaged propaganda
or "entertainment"); in spite of the fact that we no
longer have any illusions when we consider person-
ages such as Brecht or Benn—in short, within the
framework of our spontaneous attitude toward
poetry, there remains nevertheless one element
entirely unaffected, an element clearly tending to
side with Plato and his thesis. This element obviously cannot be attacked and eliminated either
through our acquaintance with degenerate poetry
or through any dose of analytical and caustic criti-
cism. In all the reflective meditation on poetry, even
as its result, this element every now and then comes
to the fore. This fact, indeed, must most forcefully
be called to mind, to prevent us from giving in to
our immediate reaction of taking Plato's thought as
merely historical and thus dismissing it.

This particular element is attested hundreds of
times in the works of such poetic masters as Novalis
or Hölderlin. It is so self-evident that we see no
need to belabor it at any length. It is appropriate, at

any rate, to consider the unromantic precision of the following sentence in Hölderlin's "Comments on Antigone": "It is of great benefit to the soul, working in secret, that at the height of consciousness it moves away from consciousness . . . ." But it is altogether more surprising to hear a rational thinker such as Lessing declare about his own creations that it would be too much of an honor to call them "poetry" and himself "a poet": "That living spring—I do not feel it inside myself . . . ." Similar utterances came from Adalbert Stifter, always so level-headed; he says that "at no time did [he] regard [his] own writings as poetry", nor would he "ever presume . . . to call them poetry. There are very few poets in this world." The impressive realism of Goethe, the great writer of letters, is not content with such merely negative characterizations. He offers all but Platonic formulations: "The poet is in fact out of his senses"; and "in keeping with the humble truth, he has to admit that his condition is altogether a trance between waking and dreaming; in effect, I do not deny that many a thing appears to me like a dream . . . ." As the "main prerequisite for true poesy" he lists "an overwhelming nature, an irresistible urge, an insistent passion". Is not all of this simply another description of the same poetic *mania* discussed by Plato in his *Phae-drus*?

And yet, there is no need to dig into the past. Even a poet such as Gottfried Benn, who clearly loved to destroy, with a heavy hand and with his Berlinesque diction, any romantic atmosphere ("a poem very rarely 'comes about'; a poem is made"), even Benn is completely aware of the compulsion involved in poetic creation, a compulsion that can neither be controlled rationally nor avoided. Many explicit remarks to the contrary notwithstanding, he expresses in specific words the very elements of the *theia mania*, the being-beside-oneself rooted at least beyond the human sphere: "The essence of poetry is perfection and fascination . . . that such perfection exists in and of itself, this I do not affirm." It sounds rather grotesque, really, when Max Rychner declares, in his epilogue to Gottfried Benn's *Selected Letters*: ". . . his evening ritual of walking to the neighborhood tavern, with its lowly, populous loneliness, resulted in some kind of incantation, when he, totally absorbed into himself, became a mystic, and his beer stein a chalice." Nevertheless, I think this is probably an accurate description of the inner reality.

After all, this is an experience that might happen to anybody; at the very moment we are touched and moved by the voice of genuine poesy in the creations of Gottfried Benn, or Franz Kafka, or Georges Bernanos, we know that it is not the two insurance agents Kafka and Bernanos to whom we ascribe any such authority. The cliché—stale by now—of saying "according to the poet" is not entirely mistaken! Of course, who would this "poet" be, if not the dermatologist Dr. Benn? We will certainly not go so far as to claim a divine voice speaking simply and directly through the medium of the poet. And yet, would we consider ourselves to be completely correct if we affirmed that the intense emotional power of great poetry is entirely without any connection to the ultimate, all-embracing divine foundation of the world? This precisely is the question Plato challenges us to face when he speaks of the poet's divine *mania*.

EROS

FINALLY, SOCRATES SPEAKS of the erotic experience, through which we humans, if circumstances are rightly ordered and favorable, can also encounter and expect something healing, enriching, even divine.

This means, not that every infatuation between any Jack and Jill is *eo ipso* a divine gift, but that in every erotic emotion there is contained the possibility, the context, and the promise of something reaching infinitely beyond its immediate significance. Yet man will truly partake of the promised gift only on condition that, when receiving the impetus born of emotion, he accepts and sustains it in lasting purity. In this context, the possibilities of corruption, adulteration, dissimulation, pretension, and pseudo-actualization lie dangerously close—as they do, incidentally, in the case of the prophetic, the cathartic, and the poetic *mania*.

Much worse, of course, and more hopeless than
an honest "No" is a faked "Yes", when perhaps the
semblance of inner emotion is being deceptively
upheld, perchance even deceiving one's own thinking, as if there were enchantment with beauty
whereas in reality there is nothing but totally un-
emotional, calculating craving for pleasure. Nonetheless, Plato holds that for the true lover a gift
awaits that is entirely comparable to what man
receives in divine revelation, in *catharsis*, and in
poetic inspiration.

Goethe, after having discussed, in *Dichtung und
Wahrheit* [Poetry and Truth], his own erotic experiences, states the same: "The sincere loving yearnings
of uncorrupted youth take quite a spiritual turn.
Nature seems so to arrange things that one gender
would sensibly perceive in the other whatever is
good and beautiful. Thus when I beheld this
maiden, when my heart yearned for her, a whole
new world of beauty and excellence unfolded
before me." It is an evil thing when lustful desire
comes before erotic emotion, suffocating it! "As
soon as lust intrudes, love cannot claim perma-
nence"—so wrote André Gide in his diary.

To make this point evident is the intent of the discourse that now follows in Plato's *Phaedrus*. At the

outset, however, he states that this discourse will indeed sound convincing to the wise yet unconvincing to the "clever". The Greek term employed here is *deinós*, which in our dictionaries is rendered as "dreadful, terrible, tremendous", as well as "powerful, efficient, exceptional". Obviously, something is meant here that is at one and the same time admirable, astonishing, and terrifying; and such can indeed be ascribed, justifiably, to the "purely rational mind". A clever man, Socrates states, will always consider unconvincing the notion that true lovers, in their being-beside-themselves, are promised and might receive a divine gift.

But then, Socrates starts all over again, and the theme of "Eros" seems at first to get hopelessly lost. "Before anything else," he says, "we must investigate the truth with regard to the nature of the soul, by observing its conditions and powers." Someone else had once begun a discourse on Eros in the same manner—namely, Aristophanes, in Plato's *Symposium*: "Before anything else", that is, before you can say anything substantial about Eros, you must know the nature of man and reflect on all that has affected it (*pathémata*).

To answer the question raised here can never be easy. And Plato's multi-layered explanation makes use, of course, of the "ancient lore", preserved in the mythical tradition. "Thus do I begin my demonstration", we read in *Phaedrus*; "every spiritual being is immortal". The things we are familiar with do not prepare us for Plato's notion of immortality, which refers not only to the future but to the past as well. The human soul—this is his meaning—is not only without end but also without beginning, *agénetos*.

We are wont to disregard this idea, for it appears alien to us and outside our customary thinking, as something above all incompatible with the Christian and Western concept of the human soul. And yet, does not the Christian doctrine in the end agree with this Platonic notion? We, too, conceive of the spiritual soul as something that, strictly speaking, does not "become". The theological teaching that the human soul, like every spiritual being coming into existence, is directly "created" contains without doubt the correct insight that, unlike everything else, which "develops" and "unfolds", the soul does not actually "originate". A "genesis" of the soul would be inconceivable.

This thesis, by the way, has a direct contemporary relevance; it does not merely approximate Plato's concept, it obviously expresses the very same thought! This sameness is being underlined here not

for the purpose of forcing it into some modern per-
tinency, but in order to prevent the contemporary
student of Plato from thinking that such reading
exercises, perhaps dealt with to the point of weari-
ness, are by now only of historical interest and
hence no longer relevant. Plato's genius manifests
itself in the very fact that his insights cannot easily
be dismissed, even though their verbal expression
may seem questionable. They have kept their relevance, and we are unable to replace them with
insights more pertinent.

The same applies to Plato's philosophical dictum
that the natural habitat of the soul is the universe of
all that exists. Even though we do not appropriate
Plato's formulation that the soul "reigns throughout
the entire cosmos", we cannot, on the other hand,
bring ourselves to understand and describe the spirit
as anything but an essence whose nature includes
existing within the universal horizon of all there is.
"To be endowed with spirit" means specifically this:
to be dealing with all there is. As Thomas Aquinas
formulated it: the nature of this spirit is manifested
first and foremost in its *convenire cum omni ente*
(affinity with all that is).

Plato tried to gain some insight into the primordial accidents and fates that befell the soul by

employing several illustrations, which, in the end, all bring out the same idea: that man has lost, through his own offense, the perfection originally reserved for him as part of his supernatural destiny and that, in consequence, he is now incessantly chasing after the original ideal form. The primordial condition, being at the same time the true goal and end of human existence, constitutes the object of man's *remembrance* as well as his *longing*. However, both remembrance and longing can unfold only if man, be it ever so briefly, leaves behind the busyness of his activities and steps outside the concerns of his workaday world.

And so, finally, we shall speak of *eros*, the *erotic mania*, the basic form of man's being-beside-himself occurring specifically in his encounter with sensual beauty. For beauty, specifically physical beauty, if man approaches it receptively, can affect and strike him more than any other "value", can push him outside the realm of his familiar and controlled environment, outside his "neatly explained world", in which he deems himself rather confidently at home, as Rilke puts it.

Common language informs us, furthermore, that beauty is above all "attractive". "Attracted", then, is he who has lost, be it only for a moment, the calm contentedness of his self-possession; he is, as we say, "moved" by something else—he has to "suffer" all this. This state, in which all orderly familiarity (together with one's self-possession) vanishes, Plato describes again and again with ever new expressions: a desire to soar on wings while being utterly unable to do so; being beside oneself while not knowing what is going on; ferment, restlessness, helplessness. We also find rather "unpoetic" comparisons; for instance, Socrates speaks of the uncomfortable condition of a child who is teething. The lovers—this we read in Aristophanes' speech in the *Symposium*—do not know what they ultimately desire of each other; it is rather evident that their souls yearn for something other than the mere pleasures of love. This "other", however, the soul is unable to name: "It has only some vague idea about the true object of its desire, and its own explanations are but riddles."

At this point something important comes into view: the difference between desire and love. He who desires knows clearly what he wants; at heart he is calculating, entirely self-possessed. Yet desire is not the same as love; the one being loved is, in a strict sense, not the one who is being desired but the one for whom something is desired. He who loves in such a non-desiring way, however, does not determine his actions or initiatives all by himself; rather, he is "being moved" when contemplating the beloved. Whatever is being loved most and moves us most, as Plato states, is beauty, for which reason those who love beauty are called simply "lovers".

We latter-day, enlightened readers of Plato are all too ready to consider such a discourse to be overly emotional, unrealistic, and romantic. Yet I believe this would be a mistake. Plato's discourse is entirely rational; he has no illusions about the fact that much, if not most, of what generally passes for "love" is nothing but desire. He knows that true rapture enticed by beauty occurs only rarely. Plato insists, however, that this rare event alone actualizes the essential purpose of all human encounter with beauty. "Few there are who remember . . . the sacred things they once beheld."

Nothing evokes this remembrance more intensely than beauty; this is a specific characteristic of beauty. In its power to lead toward a reality beyond the here and now, beyond immediate perception, it cannot be compared to anything in this world. Anyone who has some understanding of Plato's philosophy will know that, in his conception, whatever we experi-

ence in this world as real, true, and good is but a
reflection, that is, something pointing to an arche-
type not directly observable. Still, we may encounter
embodiments of goodness, justice, or wisdom—no
matter to what degree of perfection, perhaps in the
person of a just ruler—such that it would be almost
impossible not to react with admiration and devo-
tion. Such experiences nonetheless do not have the
power to enrapture us; they do not transport us
beyond the here and now. Beauty alone can accom-
plish this; only the encounter with beauty evokes
remembrance and yearning, prompting in the one so
touched the desire to get away from the course of all
those things that usually absorb the human mind.

This distinctive essence of beauty is described by
Plato on two levels: the level of otherworldly experience (beauty "beyond" this space and time) and
the level of the present existence (beauty here and
now).

Plato is obviously unwilling to conceive of the
ultimate perfection in store for man in terms other
than the encounter with divine *beauty*, not as
encounter with the idea of the "good", or of
"being", or of anything else. To illustrate this point,
we have only to quote a few lines from Diotima's
speech in the *Symposium*: Toward this end of his

journey, he will see "a wondrous vision, beautiful in its nature. . ."; beautiful not "in the guise of a face or of hands or any other portion of the body . . .", but as primordial beauty, "existing ever in singularity of form independent by itself . . ."! Are you not convinced that at that point he "is destined to become the beloved of the gods"? And in the Dialogue *Phaedrus* we read: "At that time" (linguistically, this expression denotes the past, including the primordial past, as well as the future, including the eschatological future), "at that time, we, for our part, followed in this band of Zeus . . . and beheld that blissful sight and spectacle, and were initiated into that mystery, which by eternal right is pronounced the most blessed of all mysteries . . . beauty, beheld at that time in its shining splendor."

Even on the level of our earthly existence, beauty is something incomparably exceptional. It is the one thing most eminently visible; we perceive beauty through our eyes, the most light-filled of our senses. *Pulchrum est quod visu placet*—beautiful is that which pleases the eye of the beholder. This is a straightforward answer; neither a scent, nor a taste, nor anything tangible, not even a special sound can, in the strict sense, be called a thing of "beauty". No other spiritual reality comes before our eyes with such immediate visibility. Wisdom, for instance, cannot be "seen". Plato adds here, if wisdom were as visible to our eyes as beauty is, "then a fearsome love would nigh be enkindled", a love apt to upset and destroy our existential structure, to transport us in total rapture outside our earthly existence. Neither wisdom nor anything else worthy of love but "only beauty was destined to be most visible and most lovable at the same time".

Plato, to repeat, does not hold that beauty moves man's inner core inevitably and, as it were, automatically, without fail; not even that this happens with regularity—he is very much aware that beauty may well awaken an irreverent, selfish desire. Only those who open up to remembrance will be shaken to their core. Like gentle rain passing through the windows of the eyes, beauty prompts the soul to sprout wings again, to soar to the dwelling of the gods, from where the soul originated. In this very experience, in the opinion of Plato's Socrates, the nature of Eros is experienced and activated. For this reason do the gods call Eros not the "winged one" but the "wing-giver", an expression Plato quotes from an ancient poem.

The essence of beauty, therefore, if what has been said here is true, precisely does not consist in providing satisfaction, like something that "gratifies", no matter how highly spiritual a gratification it may be. Goethe, rather surprisingly, captured this Platonic notion in an admirably succinct sentence: "Beauty is not so much a fulfillment as rather a promise." In other words, by absorbing beauty with the right disposition, we experience, not gratification, satisfaction, and enjoyment but the arousal of an expectation; we are oriented toward something "not-yet-here". He who submits properly to the encounter with beauty will be given the sight and taste not of a fulfillment but of a promise—a promise that, in our bodily existence, can never be fulfilled.

This last formulation in turn closely echoes a quotation found in Paul Claudel's writings: Woman is "the promise that can never come to pass: this very fact constitutes my grace." Claudel's statement, as well as Goethe's, seems to express accurately the thought of Plato, who holds that the deep erotic emotion tied to the encounter with beauty is a form of *theia mania*, the god-given being-beside-oneself, insofar as the actual occurrence does not produce a "fulfillment"—any satisfaction in dwelling here and now—but instead entices our inner existential space to reach for some infinite fulfillment not available here and now except by way of yearning and remembrance. He who in contemplation of earthly beauty remembers the one true beauty "again sprouts wings . . ."; and thus the true lover, long before our common exile has lapsed, is transported into communion with the gods.

And this, indeed, is said not only of the lover but of the philosopher! This connection, at first sight rather puzzling, is found also in the *Symposium*. This is not the place to discuss it in detail, yet at the very least we must notice that Plato here is not thinking at all of something non-committal and poetic; on the contrary, he envisions something very specific. Lovers and philosophers are connected by special ties, insofar as both erotic excitement and genuine philosophical quest trigger a momentum that, in this finite existence, can never be stilled. In an encounter with sensual beauty, if man opens up totally to the object of the encounter, a passion is born that, in the realm of the senses, which at first would seem to be the only adequate realm, can never be satisfied. The same holds true for the first moment of philosophical wonder (the wonder that arises from our contact with "reality"); a question arises that, in our finite world—which may mean, for example, with the tools of "science"—will also never receive an answer. The philosopher and the true lover—neither will find fulfillment except through a divine favor.

If, in retrospect, you consider the core of what has been said, you may be tempted to conclude that all this, while admittedly impressive, is at the same time an "ideal" concept that hardly applies to the reality of any living and breathing human being. It is pointless to argue with such an impression. Everything depends on how one defines human "reality" and a "genuine" human being.

Incidentally, Plato does not in fact make a series of apodictic assertions. He simply describes a possibility. His own conviction, however, is clear: Man has the capacity to experience in erotic emotion, accepted and sustained with purity—and possibly in no other context—a unique promise pointing to a fulfillment more deeply satisfying than any fulfillment in the realm of the senses. And this, too, is asserted in Plato's *Phaedrus* as indisputable fact: only when this happens has the true meaning of "eros" become manifest.

How little danger there is for Plato to stray and lose touch with real life is shown, in the *Phaedrus*, in the closing passages of Socrates' speech. This text is so astonishing that Wilamowitz himself is at a loss for words to express his surprise; these closing passages, he says, simply represent a contradiction to everything Plato has otherwise taught.

A close scrutiny of the text shows that Socrates (Plato) speaks of four different experiences in which *eros* is figured or disfigured.

The first form he mentions is the brutality of the many who desire nothing but pleasure in the most vulgar sense of the word. No trace here of romanticizing and disregarding reality!

In second place he discusses the refined sensuality of a rational hedonism, which in essence aims at pleasure alone.

The third form is an *eros* that renounces pleasure, being love's heroic fullness and its most blessed reality. Those whose love is of this kind will, upon their death, leave this earthly life, "as if on wings and without oppressing burden"; they will be able to rise at once aloft to the divine sphere, again to participate in the heavenly procession and the great banquet of the gods.

Most astonishing, however, is the *Phaedrus*' discussion of the fourth form of *eros*. Socrates speaks of love that is not entirely continent, yet at the same time is not mere craving but true loving yearning, enchantment, self-giving, and non-calculating rapture. Those possessed by this kind of love, we are told, will gain no mean victory trophy, thanks to their *mania*, their readiness to rise above their own selfishness. When they die, the soul will leave the body not with perfect wings but, at least, with sprouting ones. Because the soul had already set foot on the path of the heavens, it will not get lost in darkness. Most clearly, this is meant in an eschatological sense; the notion of "salvation" is involved; and "salvation" takes place only—but also always—in circumstances where true love is present. Cast into perdition, into darkness, is that form of "rationality" which, "greedily calculating, assigns earthly and imperfect things to the soul, thus breeding in it only vulgarity".

The learned literature on Plato asks in amazement where else in the Platonic Dialogues "we can find such leniency toward the weaknesses of the flesh". This question, I think, entirely misses the substance of the discussion. The point is not that Plato would have excused here sins stemming from the weakness of the flesh. Rather, it is stated that such weakness can be compensated, even transformed—through the wing-giving power of true love.

Modern man, a Christian especially, may at first find it rather strange that the powers attributed to "true love"—namely, the ability to "remember" and the wing-giving capacity of eros, leading back to the dwelling of the gods—should reside in such closeness to what is physical, sensual, even biological. And yet, this Platonic thought is not really foreign to Christianity's traditional moral notions; on the contrary, we find there its clear parallel. Thomas Aquinas is equally convinced that neither "elevated" nor "spiritual" love—neither *dilectio*, resulting from a conscious choice of the will, nor *caritas*, based on divine grace—can become a living reality without the *passio amoris*, that is, without the soul's being moved by a concrete sensory presence. True, this view does not necessarily imply that elevated and spiritual love is no more than the progression or "sublimation" of the erotic *passio*; without doubt, Thomas would insist rather that an elevated and spiritual love is capable of purifying and controlling this *passio amoris*. Still, this great *magister* of Christianity, not unlike Plato, is of the opinion (difficult to explain to a "Christian" consciousness prone to embrace Manichaeism and spiritualism) that *caritas*, when cut off from the vital root of the *passio amoris*, can neither come about as a truly human act nor endure in living expression.

This conviction is by no means only of theoretical importance for a conceptual definition of human nature. Indeed, it finds its clear verification time and again in the experiences of the psychoanalytical profession. Such experiences, for instance, reveal that the aggressive suppression of a person's potential for sensual, erotic emotions makes love *as such* impossible and also suffocates *dilectio* and *caritas*. Similarly, the intolerance, the harshness, and the stubbornness often found in people who claim to be very "spiritual" could well be the result of an unnatural suppression of the *passio amoris*. Man, even in his most sublime spirituality, is always an incarnate being. This bodily reality, which makes each person either a man or a woman, even on the highest level of spiritual life, does not constitute simply a barrier and a limitation; it is at the same time the beautiful wellspring of all human activity. On this, Thomas Aquinas and Plato thoroughly agree.

One other "discrepancy", much discussed, between Plato's concept of *eros* and what the Christian sees as the truth turns out to be, when closely examined, of no consequence. Plato's notion of *eros*, it is said, amounts in this end to nothing more than a selfishness that aims to enrich and satisfy the self, while the Christian idea of *caritas* and *agape*, in contrast, means a love that is generous, unselfish, and giving. To construct such a contrast, in itself already

an almost inadmissible simplification, invites ready
challenges from both sides of the question. For one,
eros, ascending to the contemplation of archetypal
beauty, will also, in Plato's conception, be transformed into an attitude that leaves far behind all
selfish desires and is most appropriately called a
form of "worship". The conclusion of Diotima's
discourse in the *Symposium* can hardly be inter-
preted differently.

Above all, moreover, it is questionable whether
man is at all capable of a totally "unselfish" love.
Christian theology, too, defines the highest form of
caritas as that state in which God is loved as the
source of all bliss. Such bliss, however, which ultimately is the quest of all love, is nothing other than
the final quenching of man's most profound thirst.
Man is by nature a being that thirsts and yearns, and
not only because he "moves in the world of the
senses", as Kant has it, but precisely insofar as he is
spirit. To be so "unselfish" as to be ready to re-
nounce the ultimate fulfillment, eternal bliss, is
entirely impossible for us. Our will, as Thomas
Aquinas has formulated many times, is unable *not* to
desire such bliss.

CONCLUSION

IT IS EASY to see that our discussion here covers questions of striking relevance. To appreciate this point, one has only to focus on a certain understanding of man that already appears on the horizon of our possibilities, a type of man who says: We do not need any supernatural answers; we ourselves take care of any psychological problems that call for relief; any "art" that neither satisfies a specific need, even if this need is only entertainment, nor serves the political and technological control of the world is not welcome; and above all, sexuality must not be hindered in its expressions or idealized romantically.

It is quite evident that the present time especially cries out for a keener awareness of the Socratic-Platonic wisdom as discussed in this essay. It cries out for resistance to the attempt and the temptation to establish the autocratic rule of man, who deludes himself that he possesses sovereign powers over the world and over himself and thus squanders his real existential patrimony.

Such patrimony is achieved and preserved only through a willingly accepted openness: openness for divine revelation, for the salutary pain of *catharsis*, for the recollecting power of the fine arts, for the emotional shock brought about by *eros* and *caritas*—in short, through the attitude rooted in the mysterious experience that Plato called *theia mania*.

Translator's Note

I have tried to render direct quotations according to an acknowledged English source, thereby at times slightly deviating from the German text.

English versions used:

Plato, *Symposium*, trans. W. R. Lamb (Cambridge, Mass./London, 1975)

Plato, *Phaedrus*, trans. J. Wright

Virgil, *Aenead*, trans. Robert Fitzgerald

T. S. Eliot, *The Family Reunion,* in *The Complete Poems and Plays: 1909–1950* (New York, 1952)

C. S. Lewis, *The Screwtape Letters* (New York, 1944)